SHANE MACGOWAN'S MELODY: A JOURNEY THROUGH THE PUNK-FOLK SYMPHONY

Behind the Lyrics: Unmasking the Soul of The Pogues' Frontman

Shane MacGowan's Melody: A Journey Through the Punk-Folk Symphony

Copyright © 2023 Gabriel.O All rights reserved

The characters and events portrayed in this book are nonfictional. Any similarity to real persons, living or dead, is not coincidental and it's intended by the author.

No part of this book may be reproduced, or stored in a retrieval system, or transmitted in any form or by any means, electronic, mechanical, photocopying, recording, or otherwise, without express written permission of the publisher.

Cover design by: Art Painter
Library of Congress Control Number: 2018675309
Printed in the United States of America

Roland T. Owens

Shane MacGowan's Melody: A Journey Through the Punk-Folk Symphony

Dedication

In the realm of storytelling, where narratives unfold like a tapestry of experiences, this biography finds its heartbeat in the life and legacy of Shane MacGowan. To you, a soul whose journey has carved indelible marks on the canvas of existence, this book is dedicated.

In the quiet moments and the vibrant chapters of your life, we discover a symphony of resilience, passion, and the pursuit of dreams. Your narrative is one of inspiration, a testament to the extraordinary potential within ordinary moments. It is an honour to weave the threads of your story into the fabric of these pages, hoping to capture the essence of a life lived with purpose and determination.

To the dreamers who dare to imagine beyond the horizon, this dedication extends to those who find kinship in the pursuit of greatness. Shane MacGowan, your footsteps have echoed in the corridors of achievement, reminding us that the journey is as significant as the destination.

This dedication is a tribute to the layers of your identity, the triumphs that sparkle in the sunlight and the shadows that have moulded the contours of your character. Your resilience is a beacon for those navigating their own paths, an enduring reminder that challenges are but stepping stones to triumphs yet unseen.

In the genesis of this biography, the ink of your name becomes a brushstroke, painting a portrait that transcends the boundaries of time and circumstance. As we delve into the intricacies of your experiences, many readers find inspiration in the vulnerabilities, strength in the struggles, and a shared humanity in the anecdotes that unfold.

To the family and friends who have been steadfast companions on this journey, this dedication acknowledges the support, love, and shared laughter that infuse the pages with warmth. Each chapter is a collective story, a mosaic woven by the hands of those who have walked alongside Roland T. Owens.

As we embark on this literary odyssey, it is with deep appreciation for the wisdom garnered from the chapters of your life. Your legacy extends beyond the words on these pages, resonating in the hearts of those fortunate enough to cross

Shane MacGowan's Melody: A Journey Through the Punk-Folk Symphony

paths with your story. May this dedication be a small token of gratitude for the richness you've brought to our shared narrative.

In the dance of words and the melody of memories, your name, Shane MacGowan, stands as a cornerstone. May your story inspire, uplift, and echo in the minds of readers, inviting them to reflect on their own journeys and embrace the beauty of a life well-lived.

With sincere admiration and gratitude,

Roland T. Owens

Shane MacGowan's Melody: A Journey Through the Punk-Folk Symphony

Acknowledgment

In the opening notes of "Shane MacGowan's Melody: A Journey Through the Punk-Folk Symphony," I find myself reflecting on the odyssey of bringing this biography to life. This acknowledgment is a humble offering of gratitude to the individuals and forces that have woven their influence into the tapestry of this literary exploration. As the author, Roland T. Owens, I extend my heartfelt appreciation to all who have contributed to this labour of love.

First and foremost, I express my deepest thanks to Shane MacGowan, the enigmatic protagonist of this narrative. Unravelling the layers of your life, music, and spirit has been both an honour and a privilege. Your willingness to share the nuances of your journey has not only enriched this biography but has also created a bridge for readers to connect with the soul behind The Pogues' frontman. This acknowledgment is a tribute to the authenticity you've brought to this project.

To my family, the unwavering pillars of support throughout this endeavour, your understanding, patience, and encouragement have been my compass. The late nights at the writing desk, the moments of self-doubt, and the triumphs have all been shared

Shane MacGowan's Melody: A Journey Through the Punk-Folk Symphony

experiences, and I extend this acknowledgment with deep gratitude for your constant presence.

To the editorial team, whose meticulous attention to detail has shaped this narrative, thank you for your invaluable contributions. Your insights, suggestions, and dedication to preserving the essence of Shane MacGowan's story while enhancing its clarity have played a pivotal role in bringing this biography to its fruition. This acknowledgment is a nod to your expertise and commitment to the craft of storytelling.

A special acknowledgment goes to the research team and archivists who delved into the annals of history to uncover the nuances that colour this narrative. Your dedication to accuracy and thoroughness has added depth and context to the portrayal of Shane MacGowan's life and the musical landscape of his era.

To the musicians, collaborators, and industry insiders who shared their perspectives and memories, your contributions have been instrumental in creating a comprehensive portrait of Shane MacGowan. This acknowledgment extends to your openness in sharing anecdotes, insights, and reflections that have added layers to the storytelling canvas.

Shane MacGowan's Melody: A Journey Through the Punk-Folk Symphony

To the fans and followers of Shane MacGowan, who have shared their passion and enthusiasm for his music and persona, this acknowledgment is a recognition of the community that surrounds and celebrates the artistry of this remarkable individual. Your connection to the music has breathed life into the pages of this biography, and I am grateful for the collective energy you bring to this project.

To my literary mentors and guides, your wisdom and encouragement have been beacons in navigating the challenges of bringing a complex biography to fruition. This acknowledgment is a salute to your generosity in sharing knowledge and fostering a love for storytelling.

The acknowledgement extends to the team behind the scenes, the designers, publicists, and everyone who played a role in bringing "Shane MacGowan's Melody" to the hands of readers. Your collaborative efforts have transformed words on paper into a tangible, immersive experience.

To the individuals who may not find their names on these pages but have left an indelible mark on the journey of creating this biography, I extend my collective appreciation. The web of influence is vast, and this acknowledgment is an

Shane MacGowan's Melody: A Journey Through the Punk-Folk Symphony

acknowledgment of the interconnectedness that shapes creative endeavours.

As I release "Shane MacGowan's Melody" into the world, this acknowledgment is not just a formality but a sincere expression of gratitude. It is an acknowledgment of the collective effort, passion, and dedication that have shaped this exploration of a musical odyssey. May this biography resonate with readers, inviting them into the symphony of Shane MacGowan's life and leaving them with a deeper appreciation for the melodies that define his legacy.

With heartfelt thanks,

Roland T. Owens

Shane MacGowan's Melody: A Journey Through the Punk-Folk Symphony

"In the cadence of life, each melody weaves a tale, a symphony of joy, sorrow, and the undying spirit of rebellion. In the echoes of Shane MacGowan's music, we find not just notes but a narrative that transcends time, inviting us to dance to the rhythm of our own unique stories."

Shane MacGowan's Melody: A Journey Through the Punk-Folk Symphony

Preface

In the world of biographies, the canvas upon which we paint the lives of extraordinary individuals is as vast and complex as the stories themselves. "Shane MacGowan's Melody: A Journey Through the Punk-Folk Symphony" is not merely a recounting of events; it is an exploration, a melody echoing through the corridors of time, inviting readers to venture into the heart and soul of one of music's most iconic figures.

As the author, Roland T. Owens, I stand at the threshold of a narrative that has been both a labour of love and a compelling voyage into the realms of punk-folk history. Shane MacGowan's story, rich and multifaceted, unfolds not just as a biography but as a tapestry woven with threads of rebellion, passion, and the timeless allure of music.

Before we delve into the nuances of Shane MacGowan's life, let us cast our gaze back to the late '70s—the tumultuous landscape where punk-folk found its birth. It is here that our protagonist emerges, a pivotal figure in a musical revolution that would challenge conventions and redefine the very essence of folk music. In the opening chapters, we set the stage, immersing ourselves in the cadence of an era marked by rebellion, cultural

Shane MacGowan's Melody: A Journey Through the Punk-Folk Symphony

clashes, and the birth pangs of a genre that would echo through the decades.

The central theme that reverberates through the pages of this biography is the exploration of the soul behind The Pogues' frontman. Shane MacGowan, with his raw lyricism and unapologetic authenticity, becomes the lens through which we examine the intricate interplay of life, lyrics, and legacy. Each chapter peels back layers, delving into the formative experiences, the roots of rebellious spirit, and the collaborative energy that defined The Pogues.

As we navigate through the narrative, a journey unfolds, a journey that mirrors the evolution of MacGowan's life, career, and musical prowess. From the early days of punk-folk fusion to the refined symphony that would captivate global audiences, we trace the footsteps of a musical pioneer. The exploration extends beyond the melodies to the very heart of MacGowan's songwriting process, dissecting the elements that constitute his poetic toolkit.

Yet, the melody of Shane MacGowan's life is not confined to the stage. It resonates through the tumultuous chapters of personal struggles, addressing challenges and triumphs that influenced his

Shane MacGowan's Melody: A Journey Through the Punk-Folk Symphony

artistry. Substance abuse, a complex relationship with personal demons, and moments of resilience all become integral notes in the symphony of his life. We navigate through these landscapes, seeking to understand the cathartic nature of his music and the indomitable spirit that fueled his creative journey.

Beyond the music, we explore the broader cultural impact of MacGowan's unapologetic authenticity and rebellious image. His influence reverberates through realms of fashion, lifestyle, and societal norms, challenging established ideals and contributing to a redefinition of cultural standards. We examine how his legacy extends beyond the confines of music, becoming a cultural archetype of resilience and nonconformity.

The exploration concludes by tracing MacGowan's influence on subsequent generations of musicians, illuminating the enduring legacy he crafted within and beyond The Pogues. From pioneering punk-folk fusion to influencing diverse genres, MacGowan's impact becomes a timeless musical archetype. The collaborative spirit, cultural impact, and thematic resonance of his work leave an indelible mark, transcending temporal and genre boundaries.

Shane MacGowan's Melody: A Journey Through the Punk-Folk Symphony

As the author of this biography, I undertook a journey into the heart of punk-folk history and the life of Shane MacGowan with profound reverence. The writing process became a symphony of its own—a delicate dance between research, reflection, and storytelling. The goal was not just to recount events but to capture the essence of a man whose music transcends genres, leaving an indelible mark on the cultural landscape.

In navigating the complexities of MacGowan's life, I found myself constantly challenged to balance the rawness of reality with the lyrical beauty of storytelling. The intricacies of his character, the nuances of his experiences, and the legacy he crafted required careful consideration. Each word was chosen with the intention of conveying not just information but the emotional depth that underscores MacGowan's musical legacy.

This preface serves as an invitation—to fellow music enthusiasts, ardent fans, and those curious about the transformative power of art. It beckons readers to step into the world of Shane MacGowan, to listen not only to the melodies but to the stories they tell. As we embark on this journey, may the pages of "Shane MacGowan's Melody" resonate with the same passion, rebellion, and authenticity that define the music it seeks to unravel.

Shane MacGowan's Melody: A Journey Through the Punk-Folk Symphony

So, with this prelude, I invite you to immerse yourself in the punk-folk symphony that is Shane MacGowan's life—a journey through the melodies that transcend time and leave an indelible mark on the pages of music history.

Roland T. Owens

INTRODUCTION

ECHOES OF REBELLION

The music environment saw a sea change in the late 1970s, characterised by experimentation, revolt, and a blending of genres. Punk-folk emerged during this period, a vibrant and nonconformist musical landscape that would give rise to a number of distinctive voices, Shane MacGowan being one of the most notable.

THE LANDSCAPE OF PUNK FOLK: A CULTURAL CAULDRON

There was a noticeable dissatisfaction and disillusionment with the way the 1970s played out. Disillusioned with society at large, the youth looked for a different way to express themselves that was in line with their rebellious nature. The raw energy, DIY mentality, and anti-establishment mindset that defined punk rock as it emerged. Meanwhile, there was a growing resurgence of interest in folk music, especially in its unadulterated, traditional form.

Shane MacGowan's Melody: A Journey Through the Punk-Folk Symphony

This unlikely union of punk and folk was born out of a mutual longing for genuineness and a rejection of the polished, mass-market music that was taking over the radio. Artists who aimed to combine the storytelling traditions of folk music with the rawness of punk found a fertile footing in the punk-folk scene.

THE ORIGINS OF POP CULTURE ICONS

This was the setting in which Shane MacGowan became a key figure. Being a native of London, the hub of the punk movement, MacGowan was well aware of the cultural changes taking place all around him. He was greatly influenced by the punk mentality of questioning the established quo, but he was also influenced by the rich legacy of Irish folk music, which would ultimately determine his creative identity.

A diverse range of inspirations typified the punk-folk scene. Reggae elements were being included by artists such as The Clash, while traditional Irish folk music was being infused with punk energy and attitude by groups like The Pogues, lead by MacGowan. A sound that was profoundly ingrained in cultural tradition and rebellious was produced by this combination.

SHANE MACGOWAN: A PIONEER OF PUNK FOLK

It becomes evident as we go deeper into this late '70s punk-folk scene that Shane MacGowan was a pioneer rather than just a participant. His first major break came with the punk band The Nips, who played in tiny clubs and put out their own CDs. They epitomised the DIY attitude of punk. However, MacGowan's musical selections and lyrical approach suggested a more expansive vision that went beyond punk convention.

MacGowan used the punk-folk scene as a canvas to convey the complexities of his identity. It was a protest against musical conventions as well as against social norms. MacGowan was able to create a sound tapestry that was both violent and introspective by fusing the energy of punk with the storytelling tradition of folk.

THE IMPACT OF CULTURE AND THE FREEDOM OF ART

Punk-folk in the late 1970s was a phenomenon in culture as much as a musical style. Artists looking for authenticity and a break from conventional sound found refuge in it. The movement made a wider variety of perspectives heard by

Shane MacGowan's Melody: A Journey Through the Punk-Folk Symphony

upending the music industry's pre-existing ideas about what qualifies as "commercial" music.

Shane MacGowan saw artistic freedom in this cultural environment. It was a playground where trying new things was not just encouraged but welcomed. His early work, which combined punk and folk elements, served as a springboard for The Pogues' eventual breakthrough, which saw them hone this distinctive sound and win over fans all over the world.

It's important to set the scene by providing an overview of the late '70s punk-folk scene in order to comprehend Shane MacGowan's early years. It was a period of musical experimentation, cross-pollination of cultures, and rebellion. This background serves as the setting for the emergence of MacGowan's unique voice as a rebel and songwriter. His voyage through this punk-folk symphony would mould his career and leave a lasting impression on the wider music scene.

Few people throughout the history of music have had as much of an impact and as much pivoting as Shane MacGowan. MacGowan became a star when the turbulent late 1970s gave rise to a musical revolution, permanently altering the punk-folk

Shane MacGowan's Melody: A Journey Through the Punk-Folk Symphony

scene and adding his name to the annals of rebellious musical brilliance.

THE ODYSSEY OF THE REBEL STARTS

Shane Patrick Lysaght MacGowan was born on Christmas Day, 1957, in Kent, England. His life would have a profound impact well beyond the borders of his birthplace. His early years suggested the rebellious spirit that would characterise his journey through the music revolution, as evidenced by his insatiable thirst for artistic expression.

MacGowan did not follow a path of uniformity. While his friends were following the traditional paths to college and work, he was making his way through London's colourful and rebellious punk scene. The metropolis, a crucible of artistic energy, served as the setting for MacGowan's transformation from a spectator to a change-agent.

THE NIPS AND THE MAVERICK'S BIRTH

With the band The Nips, MacGowan found his first voice in the punk subculture's furnace. Their unadulterated disregard of social conventions and raw energy captured the spirit of the punk movement in their songs. In addition to being a frontman, MacGowan was also a provocateur, a poet, and the usher of a new era in music.

The Nips might not have been well-known, but they did set the stage for MacGowan's rise to prominence. His incisive and reflective lyrics struck a chord with the disillusioned youth of the day, encapsulating the spirit of a generation coping with social turmoil.

THE POGUE: A SONIC CHANGE

The Pogues were the climax in MacGowan's insurrection symphony, if The Nips were the prelude. The Pogues, who were founded in 1982, embodied the union of Irish folk narrative with the raw energy of punk. Now front and centre, MacGowan's vocals would come to define the band's sound.

The Pogues were the group where MacGowan's brilliance really took off. Their groundbreaking sound design crossed genre lines and captivated listeners all around the world. The Pogues, led by the orchestrator of a sonic revolution Shane MacGowan, were a force to be reckoned with thanks to their unashamed fusion of traditional Irish folk instruments with the energy of punk.

SHANE MACGOWAN'S PENS AS SWORD: LYRICAL ALCHEMY

MacGowan's influence went well beyond only his singing abilities. With words that were equally poetic and defiant, he pierced through convention with a pen that was a formidable weapon. Whether he was exploring the intricate web of Irish tradition or the harsh streets of London, MacGowan's lyrics demonstrated his ability to capture the essence of the human condition.

Songs like "Streams of Whiskey" and "Dirty Old Town" became generational anthems, encapsulating the spirit of defiance and resiliency. Through the lyrical alchemy of MacGowan, ordinary occurrences were turned into poetic narratives, fostering an audience-artist relationship that extended beyond temporal boundaries.

UNVEILED LEGACY: BEYOND THE MUSIC

To recognize Shane MacGowan as a cultural icon in addition to his musical talents would be to introduce him as a key player in the music revolution. His unkempt look, which frequently

Shane MacGowan's Melody: A Journey Through the Punk-Folk Symphony

featured a cigarette hanging from his lips, came to represent a spirit unconstrained by social conventions. Fans responded well to MacGowan's unadulterated genuineness because they recognized a symbol of revolt and creative freedom in him.

It becomes clear that MacGowan's journey extends beyond music as we read through the various chapters of his life, from the rebellious fury of punk's early days to the folk-infused symphony of The Pogues. Beyond being a musician, Shane MacGowan is a trailblazer whose heartbreaking lyrics and raspy voice paved the way for others who dared to challenge the status quo. His legacy is a monument to the enduring force of a rebel's tune, echoing through the halls of musical history.

Shane MacGowan's Melody: A Journey Through the Punk-Folk Symphony

CHAPTER 1

REVELATIONS IN VERSE

When Shane Patrick Lysaght MacGowan breathed his first air on Christmas Day 1957 in the Kent, England, hallways, he had no idea that he was about to set off on a journey that would forever alter the face of music. Shane MacGowan's early years were a tapestry woven with the threads of formative events that shaped the rebel's musical sensibility and helped redefine punk-folk.

EARLY LIFE AND BIRTH: A GLIMPSE OF KENT'S LANDSCAPE

Shane was raised in a home heavily influenced by his Irish background and culture, being the youngest of four siblings. The bucolic scenery and undulating hills of Kent offered a tranquil counterpoint to the rebellious nature that would eventually come to define MacGowan's character.

It was clear right away that Shane was meant to follow a different route. There was music, storytelling, and a strong sense of Irish identity permeating the MacGowan home. MacGowan's strong bond with his heritage was shaped by the atmosphere created by the combination of laughter from family get-togethers and traditional folk music.

ACADEMIC REBELLION: THE INITIAL SYMPTOMS OF A MAVERICK

Shane MacGowan showed early indications of the independent spirit that would define his later years in the academic world. His upbringing, which contrasted obedience with disobedience, demonstrated a critical thinking style. While peers followed traditional educational paths, MacGowan's restless mind found comfort in the thriving London underground culture.

MacGowan's rebellious instincts were stoked by the juxtaposition between the punk movement in London and the traditional school atmosphere. The early phases of his creative development were characterised by his discontent with conformity, his desire for authenticity, and the attraction of the counterculture.

MUSIC IN EDUCATION: A MELODIC TEACHING

Traditional Irish folk music played in the MacGowan home served as young Shane's melodic compass. The eerie melodies and intricate storylines of Irish ballads seeped into his mind, laying the groundwork for the masterful storytelling that would come to define him.

Nevertheless, MacGowan was hearing more than just the melodies of Irish folk music. In the music industry, the late 1960s and early 1970s saw the rise of punk, rock 'n' roll, and the counterculture's defiant spirit. MacGowan's sound palette was expanded by the symphony of influences he encountered in this diversified musical landscape.

PUNK'S CALL: REBELLION EMERGENCE

Punk rock emerged as the 1970s developed, providing a therapeutic release for the disillusioned youth. Shane MacGowan saw this genre as a deep-seated call to insurrection more than just a musical movement. Punk's raw energy, do-it-yourself attitude, and anti-establishment vibe resonated with a young artist looking for a real platform.

Shane MacGowan's Melody: A Journey Through the Punk-Folk Symphony

London, a centre of punk culture, drew MacGowan into its turbulent embrace like a magnet. His artistic rebirth was inspired by the gritty streets, the pulsating energy of underground venues, and the intensity of punk bands breaking new territory in music.

THE EARLY MUSICAL ENDEAVOURS: THE CULMINATION OF INFLUENCES

Shane MacGowan's early musical ventures were influenced by the combination of Irish folk traditions, punk's defiant mentality, and a growing counterculture. MacGowan's literary tendencies and vocal talent began to solidify in The Nips, a punk band, where he quickly found a vehicle for his creative energy.

Despite their brief existence, The Nips gave MacGowan a stage on which to express his developing artistic vision. As the band played in little venues and put out indie CDs, the rebel's melody found its first brushstrokes on a canvas.

Shane MacGowan's early childhood became the furnace where the alchemy of his artistic sensibility began, amid the landscapes of Kent, the traditions of his family, the rise of punk, and the educational rebellion. The next parts of "Shane MacGowan's

Melody: A Journey Through the Punk-Folk Symphony" will go into further detail about how these early encounters prepared the way for a rebellious musician whose rebel tune would reverberate through the hallowed halls of musical history.

A complex web of influences, including his cultural background, life events, and the vibrant musical environment of his early years, moulded Shane MacGowan's love of music and his unique poetic style. Analysing these inspirations provides a deep understanding of the origins of MacGowan's musical style and the themes that underpin his rebellious melody.

THE FOLKLORE OF IRELAND: A SONORAN LEGACY

MacGowan's musical heritage is deeply rooted in the intricate fabric of Irish folklore. He was raised in a home where traditional songs were treasured not only as melodies but also as symbols of culture, so he was exposed to the eerie lilt and richness of Irish storytelling. Basking in centuries of storytelling, these ancestor echoes served as the foundation for MacGowan's poetic mastery.

His songs are filled with timeless themes, evocative imagery, and poetic storytelling that all bear the influence of Irish folk.

MacGowan's affinity for Irish folk gave his music a unique resonance that connected the old with the contemporary, whether he was narrating melancholic tales or channelling the spirit of revolt.

THE SOUNDS OF A GENERATION: ROCK 'N' ROLL REBELLION

The emergence of rock 'n' roll and the counterculture in the late 1960s and early 1970s caused a seismic upheaval in the music industry. A generation looking for an escape from convention connected with the rebellious spirit of bands like The Doors and The Rolling Stones. During his early years, MacGowan was exposed to the songs of defiance that defined this period.

Rock 'n' roll's electric energy and defiance of social conventions served as a trigger for MacGowan's personal revolt. The raw, unrestrained energy of his early works is evident in the impact of these rock pioneers, laying the groundwork for the punk-folk fusion that would define his later career.

Shane MacGowan's Melody: A Journey Through the Punk-Folk Symphony

PUNK'S UNDERGROUND URGENCY: A SONIC UPRISING

Shane MacGowan saw punk rock's debut in the mid-1970s as a discovery and a revolution in music. An aural vehicle for rebellion, punk's raw intensity, DIY ethos, and anti-establishment spirit connected powerfully with the disillusioned youth. MacGowan embraced this aural revolution, with The Clash, The Sex Pistols, and other punk pioneers becoming the soundtrack of dissension.

Early MacGowan's musical pursuits were heavily influenced by punk, most notably his membership with The Nips. Punk's raw energy, rebellious spirit, and simple instrumentation all contributed significantly to the development of his own sound.

BOOK INSPIRATIONS: THE HEART OF A POET

Shane MacGowan took influence for his poetic style from literature, in addition to music. His passion for Irish folklore, poetry, and ancient literature gave his songs a distinctively literary quality. MacGowan's lyrics developed into poetic narratives that went beyond song conventions, surpassing the status of mere verses.

Shane MacGowan's Melody: A Journey Through the Punk-Folk Symphony

A taste for literary narrative and the poetry of writers such as Brendan Behan and William Butler Yeats enhanced MacGowan's compositions' lyrical richness. His lyrics reached a degree of sophistication not often found in the punk and folk genres thanks to this literary mix.

REALITY AND URBAN GRIT: THE STREETS AS MUSEUM

Lyrical expression found a canvas in the harsh urban landscape of London, where MacGowan got deeply involved in the emerging punk culture. His compositions were infused with the streets, the difficulties, and the lively bustle of city life, lending a dimension of realism to his storytelling. MacGowan's lyrical approach was distinguished by its urban gritty quality, which anchored his songs in the authenticity of his real-life experiences.

When these influences are examined, it becomes evident that MacGowan's love of music and his unique poetic style did not develop independently but rather resulted from the fusion of many different factors. His artistic identity was shaped in large part by literary inspirations, gritty urban life, punk music, rock 'n' roll revolt, Irish folk traditions, and literary inspirations.

Through "Shane MacGowan's Melody: A Journey Through the Punk-Folk Symphony," you'll see how these influences combine to form a distinct melodic tapestry that characterises the rebel's melody and leaves a lasting impression on the annals of music history.

Shane MacGowan's rebellious nature, like a flame that won't go out, originated from a combination of events that influenced his early childhood. His early musical activities were a powerful manifestation of the rebellious ethos that shaped his character, and this drove him to become a leading figure in the punk-folk movement. It takes a keen sense of real expression, personal disobedience, and societal revolt to understand the origins of MacGowan's rebellious attitude and how it manifested itself in his early musical career.

DISCONTENT CULTURE: A REBELLION CATALYST

Having grown up in the late 1960s and early 1970s, Shane MacGowan experienced a constantly changing world. The counterculture was questioning social conventions, and a general dissatisfaction and disillusionment was in the air. The stirrings of a rich folk tradition, MacGowan's Irish heritage, and this cultural upheaval sowed the seeds of revolt in his mind.

MacGowan's identity was formed in a crucible where the counterculture's rebellious spirit clashed with traditional beliefs. Although he was proud of his cultural heritage, it also served as a battlefield for the rebellious spirit, which wanted to reject convention and create its own route.

SCHOLARLY DISSENT: CHASING A MAVERICK JOURNEY

MacGowan used his schooling as a platform for his early dissension. He was not interested in following the crowd and instead chose to investigate London's thriving underground scene rather than follow the usual academic path. As he forged his own intellectual route outside the confines of institutional expectations, the rebellious spirit that would ultimately define his musical career became evident at an early age.

Although MacGowan did not select classrooms as his battleground, his disobedience found expression on the streets of London and the subversive appeal of punk. This dissension in education created the foundation for a way of thinking that challenged authority and looked for authenticity outside of the curriculum.

PUNK'S PROVOCATIVE CALL: THE SONIC REVOLUTION

The late '70s brought with it the explosion of punk rock, a genre that encapsulated the rebellious spirit of the era. For MacGowan, punk wasn't just a genre; it was a sonic revolution echoing the discontents of a generation. The Sex Pistols, The Clash, and the DIY ethos of punk became the anthems of rebellion, resonating deeply with MacGowan's core.

Joining the punk movement wasn't just a musical choice for MacGowan; it was a declaration of defiance against the mainstream. The raw energy, anti-establishment ethos, and the subversive nature of punk provided a sonic canvas where MacGowan could unleash his rebellious spirit with unbridled fervour.

THE NIPS: DIY REBELLION IN ACTION

The manifestation of MacGowan's rebellious spirit found its most tangible form in his involvement with The Nips, a punk band he joined in the late '70s. The Nips embodied the DIY rebellion of the punk movement, playing in small venues, releasing independent records, and rejecting the polished aesthetics of mainstream music.

As the frontman of The Nips, MacGowan's charisma and unapologetic stage presence became emblematic of the rebellious punk spirit. His lyrics, biting and introspective, reflected a worldview that challenged societal norms and revealed the authenticity of the punk ethos.

DIY ETHOS AND INDEPENDENT RELEASE: THE REBEL'S SYMPHONY UNLEASHED

The Nips released the single "Gabrielle" in 1978, showcasing MacGowan's lyrical prowess and the band's unapologetic sound. The DIY ethos of the punk movement was in full swing, and MacGowan was at the forefront, shaping a rebellious narrative that resonated with the disenchanted youth.

Shane MacGowan's Melody: A Journey Through the Punk-Folk Symphony

This independent release marked a pivotal moment where MacGowan's rebellious spirit and his musical aspirations converged. The raw, unfiltered nature of their music was a testament to a refusal to conform, a rejection of the established order, and a declaration that authentic expression would not be compromised.

LEGACY OF REBELLION: A CATALYST FOR PUNK-FOLK FUSION

The rebellious spirit that fueled MacGowan's early musical endeavours didn't dissipate with The Nips but evolved and matured. It laid the groundwork for a more intricate rebellion, one that would find its full expression in the fusion of punk's urgency with the storytelling traditions of Irish folk.

This early rebellious chapter in MacGowan's musical journey set the stage for The Pogues, a band that would become synonymous with the punk-folk movement. The rebellion that characterised his early years became a catalyst for a sonic revolution that transcended genres, leaving an enduring legacy that resonates to this day.

In examining the roots of MacGowan's rebellious spirit and its manifestation in his early musical endeavours, we unravel the narrative of a young artist who dared to defy, a rebel whose melody would echo through the corridors of punk-folk history.

Shane MacGowan's Melody: A Journey Through the Punk-Folk Symphony

CHAPTER 2

THE BIRTH OF THE POGUES: A SYMPHONY IN REBELLION

The story of The Pogues' beginnings is one of musical alchemy, serendipity, and a group spirit that knew no bounds. At the band's founding, a collaborative spirit united many inspirations to create a sound that would later be associated with the punk-folk genre. Learning about The Pogues' origins is a trip through London's cultural intersections, a meeting point of varied musical styles, and the captivating charisma of Shane MacGowan.

A MELTING POINT IN LONDON: THE CULTURAL CAULDRON

London was a thriving cultural melting pot in the early 1980s, a place where many musical styles mixed and blended together. This was the setting in which The Pogues started to take shape. The vibrant energy of the city, along with its bars and varied music scene, served as the ideal environment for a musical

Shane MacGowan's Melody: A Journey Through the Punk-Folk Symphony

experiment that would eventually produce a distinctive sound identity.

Punk had already made a lasting impression on London, and there was still a rebellious vibe about the city. But The Pogues also wanted to add a distinctive Irish folk flavour to this energy, resulting in a hybrid sound that would quickly make its mark in the annals of music history.

The catalyst for cooperation is Shawne MacGowan's vision.

Shane MacGowan, a visionary poet and provocateur whose rebellious spirit had already had an impression on the London music scene, was the driving force behind The Pogues' founding. The driving reason was MacGowan's ambition to combine the narrative traditions of Irish folklore with the unadulterated energy of punk.

MacGowan's magnetic personality and unique poetic approach created the conditions for a groundbreaking musical experience that defied expectations. His years of artistic inquiry and disobedience refined his literary sensibilities, which served as the impetus to bring other like-minded musicians into The Pogues' orbit.

Shane MacGowan's Melody: A Journey Through the Punk-Folk Symphony

MUSICAL ECLECTICISM: A COMBINATIVE OF FLUXORS

The Pogues were more than just a group of musicians; they were a diverse group of people, each with their own history in music. The combination of punk energy with traditional Irish instruments was a break from the norm and highlighted the band's inventiveness.

Folk musicians such as Jem Finer (banjo), Spider Stacy (tin whistle), and James Fearnley (accordion) added layers of instrumentation to the traditional rock arrangement, resulting in a musical tapestry that was difficult to categorise. The band's dedication to breaking limits and adopting a truly innovative musical eclecticism was evident in the eclectic blend of inspirations.

THE POGUES' TAKE OFF: INITIAL ACTS AND EFFECTS

There was excitement and interest when The Pogues appeared on the London music scene. Early concerts in intimate settings revealed a band not afraid to try new things, fusing traditional

Irish folk music's soulful rhythm with punk's intensity. The enthusiasm, genuineness, and sheer joy that emanated from the stage enthralled the audiences.

These early performances had an effect on people who weren't sitting next to each other. The Pogues soon became well-known for their unique sound and, above all, for MacGowan's skill as a lyricist. Their sound signature—a blend of folk instrumentation and defiant lyrics—made them stand out in a crowded musical field.

ALBUM DEBUT: "RED ROSES FOR ME" AND THE RECORD DEAL

The Pogues' cooperative spirit took on a more lasting shape after they signed a record contract with Stiff Records. Their powerful statement that captured their musical ethos, "Red Roses for Me," was the title of their debut album, which was published in 1984. Traditional folk songs, unique compositions, and MacGowan's raw, intensely poetic storytelling were all mixed together on the CD.

The Pogues' "Red Roses for Me" demonstrated their skill at fusing together seemingly unrelated genres. Together with

Shane MacGowan's Melody: A Journey Through the Punk-Folk Symphony

MacGowan's poetic vision, the band's collective energy produced a selection of songs that were not just a tribute to Irish folk traditions but also clearly punk in their defiant attitude.

IMPACT ON CULTURE: A SONIC REVOLUTION

Driven by a collective spirit that broke traditions, The Pogues' distinctive fusion of punk and folk sparked a sound revolution. Their cultural influence went beyond the music industry, altering ideas about folk music and inspiring musicians of later generations. The Pogues were pioneers of a brand-new musical era, not merely a band.

Discovering The Pogues' origins allows us to see how various cultural influences came together, a poet's visionary approach, and the band's creative spirit all came together to create a new sound. The ultimate result was a musical alchemy that gave rise to a sound that defied genre boundaries, establishing an enduring legacy that draws audiences attracted to the frontman of The Pogues' rebellious spirit and the band's collective energy for daring to break musical conventions.

The Pogues' charismatic frontman Shane MacGowan played a crucial influence in defining the band's sound and the direction

Shane MacGowan's Melody: A Journey Through the Punk-Folk Symphony

punk-folk was taking. His unusual vocal delivery and lyrical creativity combined with the group's cohesiveness produced a dynamic that catapulted The Pogues to legendary status in the music industry. Examining MacGowan's performance reveals a story of musical teamwork, poetic charisma, and the unwavering energy that characterised The Pogues' lead singer.

POETIC CHARISMA: SHANE MACGOWAN'S LYRICAL GENIUS

The core of MacGowan's persona as the captivating front man was his unmatched poetic brilliance. His lyrics were novels that depicted life, love, and rebellion in great detail; they were more than just songs. MacGowan's poetic skill came from a variety of sources, such as literary traditions, Irish folklore, and his personal experiences negotiating London's harsh environments.

MacGowan's lead role and his lyrics had a compelling connection. Within punk-folk, he stood out for his ability to incorporate stories into songs that encapsulated the core of the human experience. The lyrical prowess of MacGowan became the beating heart of The Pogues, whether he was narrating grim tales of city life or channelling the poignant storytelling of Irish ballads.

Shane MacGowan's Melody: A Journey Through the Punk-Folk Symphony

THE UNADULTERATED INTENSITY OF AUTHENTICITY: VOCAL DELIVERY

MacGowan conveyed the sincerity of his songs with a raw intensity in his vocal performance. His voice, expressive and worn, served as a medium for The Pogues' stories to be told. The band's performances gained viscerality from the charismatic frontman's acceptance of faults rather than conforming to traditional vocal conventions.

The band's musical arrangements worked in perfect harmony with this unorthodox singing technique. Punk's attitude of rebellion was captured by MacGowan's delivery, which alternated between being raspy and defiant. However, it also had a lyrical aspect that blended in perfectly with the traditional Irish instruments that were a part of The Pogues' soundscape.

COLLABORATION WITH THE ENSEMBLE: THE POGUES AS A MUSICAL GROUP

One thing that made The Pogues so successful was the way MacGowan and the group worked along so well. The band was more than just the frontman's supporting cast; it was a group of talented musicians who took on the challenge of fusing the intensity of punk with the subtleties of folk instrumentation. The band's unique sound was influenced by Jem Finer's banjo, James Fearnley's accordion, Spider Stacy's tin whistle, and other ensemble members.

The group's musical ability enhanced MacGowan's captivating appearance on stage. His expressive voice and the folk-inspired instrumentation worked together to create a soundscape that was soulful yet defiant at the same time. The Pogues evolved into a band whose contributions enhanced the group's whole soundscape, and MacGowan's foremanship fit very well with this cooperative vibe.

LIVE PERFORMANCES: THEATRICS AND AUDIENCE CONNECTION

The captivating foremanship of MacGowan stole the show when he performed live. He commanded audiences with a compelling, even dramatic, aspect to his stage presence. His unadulterated, unfiltered energy served as a medium for the band's communication with the audience.

MacGowan created a strong bond with the crowd by being able to live up to the emotional depth of his words. His captivating stage persona brought The Pogues' concerts to life, whether he was singing gloomy ballads or rebel songs. There was a clear synergy between MacGowan and the group, which made the music feel like a journey that the band and its fans took together.

PUNK-FOLK IMPACT: REDEFINING GENRES

Punk-folk has never been the same since MacGowan's enchanting turn as the frontman. The Pogues' style was defined by the combination of the rebellious energy of punk with the Irish folk storytelling traditions, with MacGowan's lyrical skill serving as an anchor. Beyond musical conventions, this genre-reinvention influenced a new generation of musicians who aimed to combine authenticity with a rebellious edge.

MacGowan's influence was felt in a wider cultural context, where it redefined the punk genre's potential and challenged preconceptions about folk music. The Pogues emerged as pioneers, and MacGowan's captivating frontman ship was crucial to this revolution in music.

Shane MacGowan's Melody: A Journey Through the Punk-Folk Symphony

LEGACY: THE PERMANENT INFLUENCE OF A FRONTMAN

The memorable frontman persona that Shane MacGowan embodied has left a lasting impression. His influence extends beyond The Pogues' era, influencing punk-folk's paths and making a lasting impression on later musical generations. His charm, literary profundity, and unadulterated honesty remain benchmarks for performers who want to find a way between musical storytelling and resistance.

By analysing MacGowan's performance, we are able to piece together not only the biography of a leader but also the story of a musical visionary whose magnetic personality and poetic brilliance helped to create a sound legacy that continues to echo through the annals of punk-folk history.

PARTNERSHIP IN SONGWRITING: A COLLECTIVE STORY

MacGowan's contribution to The Pogues stretched beyond the limelight of live performances to the group's collaborative songwriting process. MacGowan's poetic contributions served as the poetic framework around which the band's songs, which

Shane MacGowan's Melody: A Journey Through the Punk-Folk Symphony

were a communal narrative, grew. His moving storytelling and the group's masterful arrangements worked in perfect harmony to produce songs that were more than just enjoyable listens; they were moving accounts of the human condition.

MacGowan's poetic creativity flourished in the framework of a band that welcomed experimentation thanks to The Pogues' collaborative songwriting style. Whether portraying the harsh realities of city life, examining themes of love and loss, or diving into historical accounts, the band's emotive core was shaped by the words of their captivating leader.

ALBUMS AS ARTISTIC STATEMENTS: THE REALISATION OF MACGOWAN'S VISION

The Pogues' albums functioned as artistic declarations that demonstrated MacGowan's vision and the group's ability to work together. Albums like "If I Should Fall from Grace with God" and "Rum, Sodomy & the Lash" demonstrate the charismatic frontman's ability to blend a variety of inspirations into well-rounded musical excursions.

MacGowan's lyrical writing achieved new heights in "Rum, Sodomy & the Lash," creating evocative images of historical themes and personal problems. The Pogues' status as a musical legend was cemented with the album's critical and commercial success, which also transformed MacGowan from a frontman into a lyrical genius.

"If I Should Fall from Grace with God" included more aspects of world music to The Pogues' already expansive sound palette while preserving their distinctive punk-folk style. MacGowan's song "Title Track" perfectly captures the rebellious attitude and lyrical depth that characterised the charismatic frontman's contributions to the band's repertoire.

DIFFICULTIES AND DEPARTURE: AN ERA'S END

Among the difficulties MacGowan experienced as the captivating leader of The Pogues were conflicts within the band and his alcoholism. But these difficulties didn't lessen the significance of his position. An era came to an end when he departed the band in the early 1990s, but his impact persisted in influencing punk-folk culture.

TRADITION AND IMPACT: CHARISMA RESONATING THROUGH TIMES

Shane MacGowan's Melody: A Journey Through the Punk-Folk Symphony

The impact of charismatic leader Shane MacGowan goes well beyond the years that The Pogues were in the public eye. His frontmanship embodied a rebellious spirit and poetic profundity that resonated with later artists, and these traits can be detected throughout his works. Thanks to MacGowan's vision, the combination of punk and folk has grown into its own genre, with artists continuing to experiment with the sound possibilities he helped create.

The captivating frontman of The Pogues not only left a lasting musical legacy but also a cultural legacy that defies expectations and honours the genuineness of artistic expression. For artists who want to imbue their music with unadulterated emotion, unreserved storytelling, and an unwavering spirit of defiance, MacGowan's magnetic energy has become an enduring source of inspiration.

By delving into Shane MacGowan's persona as the captivating leader of The Pogues, we reveal a story about a poet-king who, with his lyrics and stage presence, spearheaded a revolution in music. His magnetic personality, poetic brilliance, and collaborative nature have carved a lasting legacy in the annals of punk-folk, creating a legacy that reverberates through the ages and down the halls of musical history.

Shane MacGowan's Melody: A Journey Through the Punk-Folk Symphony

A thrilling journey through the raw, rebellious beginnings of punk-folk to a perfected symphony that would enchant listeners worldwide characterises The Pogues' sonic progression. Over the course of multiple albums, this sound transformation took place, each adding to the band's unique personality. Let's examine significant turning points in The Pogues' discography to chart the development of their music.

1. "Red Roses for Me" (1984): Punk-Folk's Origins

"Red Roses for Me," The Pogues' debut album, served as the inspiration for their distinctive punk-folk hybrid. This album, which was released in 1984, perfectly encapsulated the band's initial exuberance. Shane MacGowan broke from traditional punk and folk genres with his rebellious lyrics and folk-inspired instruments.

Songs like "Streams of Whiskey" and "Transmetropolitan" demonstrated the band's ability to eloquently combine the energy of punk with the Irish folk storytelling traditions. The raw, unrefined sound perfectly captured the punk movement's DIY mentality.

2. "Rum, Sodomy & the Lash" (1985): Historical Narratives and Maturity

The Pogues' career reached a turning point with the release of their second album, "Rum, Sodomy & the Lash," in 1985. This album, which Elvis Costello produced, showed how their music had developed. By incorporating personal problems and historical narratives into the songs, MacGowan's poetic creativity achieved new heights.

While maintaining the band's punk-folk influences, songs like "The Sick Bed of Cuchulainn" and "A Pair of Brown Eyes" showed a more sophisticated approach to composition. The Pogues gained widespread recognition and a committed following as a result of the album's success.

3. Global Fusion, "If I Should Fall from Grace with God" (1988)

The Pogues' aural palette was further extended with the release of their third album, "If I Should Fall from Grace with God," in 1988. Through the incorporation of world music elements into their punk-folk repertoire, this record represented a worldwide fusion. With its catchy melody and upbeat performance, the band's title hit became a defining anthem.

"Turkish Song of the Damned" and "Fiesta" presented a variety of musical influences, while "Fairytale of New York" demonstrated The Pogues' ability to tell intensely personal stories. The Pogues' ability to transcend genre barriers was demonstrated by the album's popularity, which cemented their appeal on a global scale.

4. "Peace and Love" (1989): Folk-Rock Fusion and Experimentation

The Pogues' experimental voyage continued with "Peace and Love," released in 1989. Folk-rock fusion was on display in the album, with songs like "White City" and "Lorelei" branching out into new musical genres. The group adopted a wider variety of musical components while adhering to their folk roots, demonstrating a more varied approach to songwriting.

The Pogues' eagerness to change and experiment with their sound was evident on this album. Their exploration of several genres offered a glimpse of the adaptability that would define their subsequent creations.

5. The 1990 song "Hell's Ditch" combines elements of rock and folk music

1990 saw the release of "Hell's Ditch," which went farther in combining rock and folk elements. Folk instrumentation and rock-infused arrangements interacted dynamically in the title track and "Sunnyside of the Street" compositions. The Pogues' musical development was continued on the album, which demonstrated their versatility in blending several styles into one cohesive whole.

6. Subsequent Records and Legacy: Polished Symphony

Later Pogues albums, such as "Waiting for Herb" (1993) and "Pogue Mahone" (1996), showcased a more sophisticated and experienced songwriting style. Even though these albums didn't have the same level of economic success as their previous releases, they cemented The Pogues' reputation as a band that could tell symphonic stories that went beyond their punk-folk roots.

The Pogues' transition from an unpolished punk-folk fusion to a polished symphony reflected the band's development and

Shane MacGowan's Melody: A Journey Through the Punk-Folk Symphony

artistic exploration. They absorbed a variety of inspirations while retaining their rebellious character, leaving a musical legacy that still has an impact on listeners all over the world. The Pogues' distinct sound is defined by the combination of punk energy, folk traditions, and a willingness to try new things. It's a symphony that enthrals listeners with its rebellious spirit and emotional depth.

CHAPTER 3

"BEHIND THE LYRICS: A POET'S TOOLKIT"

The process of producing a song by Shane MacGowan is an intriguing examination of a poetic toolkit that combines the gritty urban realism, the essence of Irish mythology, and the punk spirit of rebellion. When the layers are peeled back, the components of MacGowan's unique lyrical approach become visible, each of which adds to the complex web of stories that characterise his songwriting.

1. Street Life: Bringing Urban Grit and Realism to Life

MacGowan's poetic toolset revolves around a sharp observation of urban life. His songs frequently depict the hardships, pleasures, and complexity of living on the streets, acting as brief montages of harsh cityscapes. MacGowan's storytelling gains authenticity from his ability to convey the sense of urban grit, whether it is in the bustling streets of London or the lively bustle of city life.

2. Irish Folk Traditions: Richness of Storytelling

Drawing extensively from Irish folklore, MacGowan gives his lyrics a rich narrative quality that reflects his cultural legacy of storytelling. His use of vivid imagery, ageless themes, and a poetic style that incorporates stories into his songs is clearly influenced by traditional Irish ballads. His lyrics have a timeless aspect that bridges the past and present because of this connection to Irish culture.

3. Poetic narratives as literary inspiration

MacGowan's poetic toolset is not limited to the domain of music; it also encompasses literature. His appreciation of poetry and classic literature gives his songs a sophisticated quality. Inspired by writers such as Brendan Behan and William Butler Yeats, MacGowan transforms his lyrics into narrative poems. This literary infusion adds to the depth and complexity of his lyrics, which set his works apart in the punk-folk genre.

4. Rebellion and Social Criticism: An Intense Voice

Being a provocative voice is one of MacGowan's most distinctive poetic devices. His songs are more than just

Shane MacGowan's Melody: A Journey Through the Punk-Folk Symphony

narratives; they are also social critiques and defiant hymns that go against accepted wisdom. MacGowan's lyrics, which connect with the rebellious spirit of punk, provide a platform for dissent and a call to arms, whether addressing political issues, societal injustices, or personal struggles.

5. Romance and melancholy: A Study of the Human Condition

MacGowan explores themes of sorrow, love, and existential contemplation in his poetry, offering a sophisticated analysis of the human condition. He stands out for his ability to arouse strong emotions through moving storytelling. Songs like "Rainy Night in Soho" and "A Pair of Brown Eyes" highlight MacGowan's ability to convey the subtleties of human emotion and the intricacies of interpersonal relationships.

6. Iconic Figures and Historical Tales: Narrative Techniques

MacGowan's skill as a storyteller is demonstrated by the frequent inclusion of recognizable characters and historical tales in his songs. His skill at crafting engrossing tales, whether they are about legendary people like Cuchulainn or the creation of unforgettable characters like "Dirty Old Town," raises the storytelling quality of his lyrics above that of punk and folk music.

7. Verse Ambiguity: Appeals to Interpretation

The purposeful use of lyrical ambiguity in MacGowan's poetic toolset is an interesting feature. Many times, his lyrics are ambiguous, allowing listeners to infer their own meaning from the lines. His songs get a degree of universality from this ambiguity, which enables them to speak to a wide range of listeners and transcend particular situations.

Analysing Shane MacGowan's poetic toolkit component by component reveals a multidimensional songwriting style that embraces urban reality, draws from cultural history, integrates literary inspirations, inspires contemplation, delves into human emotions, and masters the craft of storytelling. This potent mix sums up MacGowan's poetic brilliance and adds to the lasting impact of his contributions to punk-folk music.

The words of Shane MacGowan build a mesmerising blend of urban life, Irish folklore, and introspective thoughts. His storytelling is based on this convergence, which creates a narrative environment that is deeply personal and rich in cultural depth. Let's look at how these components interact to create the unique narrative tapestry found in MacGowan's songs.

TIMELESS THEMES AND MYTHICAL ALLURE IN IRISH FOLKLORE

Irish folklore forms a fundamental part of MacGowan's poetic world. Irish tales, stories, and storytelling customs serve as a source of inspiration for him, and this is reflected in the characters and themes he uses in his lyrics. Irish folklore lends a mythical charm to his stories, as evidenced by references to Cuchulainn in "The Sick Bed of Cuchulainn" and the exploration of legendary regions.

Because of this relationship to folklore, MacGowan is able to examine universal aspects of the human condition through the prism of old tales, bringing timeless themes to the surface. These mythological components are contrasted with modern stories to produce a special blend that speaks to listeners on several levels.

DARK URBAN EXPERIENCES: STREET STORIES AND REALISM

On the other end of the scale, MacGowan's songs explore the harsh realities of city living. His writing has a realistic quality because of his astute observations of daily people's hardships, cityscapes, and street scenes. MacGowan's words create evocative images of the city, from the busy streets of "Sally MacLennane" to the bars of London.

His stories gain an authentic edge from the incorporation of gritty urban experiences, which anchor the legendary and folklore components in the real-world challenges and victories of modern life. These streetscapes are where the characters come to life, bearing the echoes of old stories while negotiating the difficulties of the concrete jungle.

PERSONAL REFLECTIONS: SENSITIVITY AND SENSUAL INTELLIGENCE

In addition to reflecting larger societal storylines, MacGowan's songs serve as a window into his own introspection. His songs frequently function as personal confessionals, sharing his own insights, wants, and challenges. Songlines such as "A Rainy Night in Soho" and "Fairytale of New York" demonstrate this intimate side, providing insights into MacGowan's inner terrain.

This intimate touch gives his narrative a level of relatability and tenderness. The songs' interwoven personal experiences and emotions, in addition to the larger themes derived from urban life and folklore, resonate with listeners.

CONVERGENCE AND INTERPLAY: A SONY COMBIENT

MacGowan's storytelling is genuinely exceptional due to the smooth interaction and convergence of these components. In his lyrics, the fantastical and the everyday, the antiquated and the modern, the global and the intensely intimate, all live in perfect harmony. His narratives are propelled by a dynamic tension created by this convergence, which permits a thorough examination of ideas and emotions.

For instance, in "Dirty Old Town," the lyrics combine a beautiful, almost dreamlike tone with a realistic portrayal of an urban setting. The "dirty old town" that serves as the title serves as a framework for introspective looks at love and desire set against an industrial gritty background.

Within "The Broad Majestic Shannon," the river functions as a symbol for Ireland's past as well as a setting for introspection.

Shane MacGowan's Melody: A Journey Through the Punk-Folk Symphony

These ideas come together to create a poetic composition that is simultaneously culturally, historically, and emotionally relevant.

By analysing the ways in which Shane MacGowan's lyrics combine urban realities, Irish mythology, and introspective thoughts, we are able to observe the skillful assembly of a narrative mosaic. Every component enhances the depth of his narrative and pushes his lyrics above accepted bounds. Characters become archetypes, locations become mythological settings, and introspective thoughts go beyond specific experiences to become timeless stories within this mosaic. A monument to the timeless power of storytelling in music, Shane MacGowan's ability to deftly combine these disparate components produces a lyrical tapestry that captivates and resonates with listeners worldwide.

An in-depth examination of the complex web of feelings and stories woven in Shane MacGowan's compositions can be obtained by using the standout tracks as case studies. His storytelling ranges from the fantastical and mythological to the realistic and intimate, as these songs demonstrate. Let's explore three standout songs, each of which is a distinct case study that showcases MacGowan's masterful lyrics.

Shane MacGowan's Melody: A Journey Through the Punk-Folk Symphony

1. The 1987 film "Fairytale of New York"

1.1 Overview: "Fairytale of New York" is among The Pogues' most well-known songs, without a doubt. It was released in 1987 and is a heartfelt, melancholy Christmas ballad with Kirsty MacColl as a duet partner. Set against the backdrop of New York City, the song captures themes of love, grief, and the harsh realities of life.

1.2 Emotional Landscape: MacGowan's "Fairytale of New York" lyrics paint a striking picture of the emotions. The conversation between the two characters—an Irish immigrant and a woman with Hollywood dreams—wavers between poignant reminiscence and hard truths. The song beautifully conveys the intricacies of interpersonal bonds, the passing of time, and the resilience of love in the face of hardship.

1.3 Layers of the Story: MacGowan's skill in developing multi-layered stories is demonstrated in this case study. The song's structure, which combines contemplation, introspection, and dialogue, gives the narrative more depth. A complex image of love that is both idealised and worn down by time is painted when the hard realities of life are contrasted with romanticised ideals.

2. 1986's "Dirty Old Town"

2.1 Synopsis: The Pogues' second album, "Rum, Sodomy & the Lash" (1985), included the iconic song "Dirty Old Town". The song is a beautiful homage to Salford, an industrial area in Greater Manchester, England. MacGowan's words elevate the commonplace to a deeply beautiful level by evoking a feeling of place and emotion.

2.2 Emotional Landscape: "Dirty Old Town" has an emotional landscape that combines romanticism and nostalgia. With its "smoky wind," "winding river," and "dirty old town," MacGowan's description of the place evokes feelings of both desire and compassion. The song's capacity to elevate the commonplace to the extraordinary accounts for much of its emotional effect.

2.3 Narrative Layers: MacGowan demonstrates his ability to paint rich pictures in this case study. The place takes on a life of its own and becomes a vehicle for the feelings portrayed in the song. As the song goes on, the narrative layers become more apparent, displaying a sense of attachment to the location and a desire for something greater—a sophisticated examination of love, connection, and the influence of one's environment.

3. The 1985 film "The Sick Bed of Cuchulainn"

3.1 Synopsis: "The Sick Bed of Cuchulainn" is a song from The Pogues' 1985 second album, "Rum, Sodomy & the Lash" The song honours the legendary Irish warrior Cuchulainn by fusing gritty urban sensibilities with folklore themes.

3.2 Emotional Terrain: In "The Sick Bed of Cuchulainn," MacGowan's words convey a sense of urgency and passion. The emotional terrain is infused with a mood of rebellion, embodying the spirit of punk and referencing the famous figure's mythic strength. The song expresses a spirit of defiance and fortitude in the face of death.

3.3 Narrative Layers: This case study demonstrates MacGowan's skill at skillfully fusing myth and fact. The storylines of "The Sick Bed of Cuchulainn" delve into Irish mythology, history, and contemplation of life's transient nature. The song develops into a sound adventure that unites the ancient and the modern by spanning space and time.

Shane MacGowan's Melody: A Journey Through the Punk-Folk Symphony

Shane MacGowan is a versatile and deep songwriter, as these case studies demonstrate. Whether MacGowan's compositions integrate myth with gritty urban reality in "The Sick Bed of Cuchulainn," explore the complexities of human relationships in "Fairytale of New York," or celebrate the beauty found in the ordinary in "Dirty Old Town," they all demonstrate a mastery of storytelling that resonates on an emotional, cultural, and historical level. His compositions leave a lasting legacy of complex emotional and narrative ties that entice listeners to become fully engrossed in the dense fabric of his poetic creativity.

Shane MacGowan's Melody: A Journey Through the Punk-Folk Symphony

CHAPTER 4

THE MAN IN THE MELODY:PERSONAL STRUGGLES AND TRIUMPHS

Shane MacGowan's artistic journey has been shaped by turbulent periods in his personal life that have included both setbacks and victories. Making sense of these experiences offers insights into the complexity that moulded The Pogues' legendary frontman.

1. The formation and early years of The Pogues (1957–1982):
Christmas Day 1957 saw the birth of Shane MacGowan in Kent, England. He had to deal with the difficulties of growing up as an Irish immigrant in England, dealing with social issues as well as cultural exile.
Due to MacGowan's love of music, The Pogues, a group that would later become influential in the punk-folk scene, were formed in 1982.

2. Ascent to Fame and "Rum, Sodomy & the Lash"
(1982–1985): During this time, MacGowan's tumultuous connection with alcohol started to show, resulting in unpredictable behaviour and moments of unreliability.
The Pogues released "Rum, Sodomy & the Lash" in 1985 to great acclaim despite personal hardships. The album was a turning point in the band's history and displayed MacGowan's poetic genius.

3. Creative Highs and Personal Difficulties (1986–1991):
MacGowan's alcoholism worsened, posing a health risk and escalating conflicts within the band.
The group kept putting out noteworthy music, such as the classic "Fairytale of New York" in 1987. The song's popularity demonstrated MacGowan's capacity to write timeless songs in spite of personal hardships.

4. Split from The Pogues (1991): MacGowan left the band due to ongoing drug problems and difficult relationships with other members.
Even after they split up, MacGowan's solo career was very successful. His 1994 album "The Snake" demonstrated his ongoing dedication to his profession.

Shane MacGowan's Melody: A Journey Through the Punk-Folk Symphony

5. Later Years and Persistent Impact (1992–2022):
MacGowan's health remained a concern, as his persistent struggles with substance misuse continued to have an effect on his well-being.

His impact persisted, and The Pogues' reputation as one of the most avant-garde punk bands was solidified. Among the many honours bestowed upon MacGowan was the 2018 Ivor Novello Award for Outstanding Contemporary Song Collection.

6. Acknowledgment and Awards (2018–2022): Health problems continued, causing mobility problems and affecting MacGowan's performance.

MacGowan was honoured for his contributions to music and culture in spite of health issues. An intimate look at Shane MacGowan's life and artistic process was given in the 2020 documentary "Crock of Gold: A Few Rounds with Shane MacGowan".

Shane MacGowan's story is one of perseverance in the face of adversity. His turbulent life, characterised by health problems and alcoholism, was balanced by a steadfast dedication to his art. The successes, which included praise and recognition in the music industry, highlighted MacGowan's lasting influence on the punk-folk subgenre. His artistic ability is still a witness to the transformational power of music in negotiating life's intricacies, even in the face of turbulent chapters.

The intricate dance of personal issues, substance misuse, and the cathartic quality of Shane MacGowan's music entwined with his artistic life. We dive into the depths of MacGowan's experiences to comprehend this complex relationship, examining how his hardships became motifs in his creative work and how the catharsis he incorporated into his music served as both a solace and a revelation.

A SYMPHONY OF TROUBLES: SHANE MACGOWAN'S TIMID JOURNEY

The depth and diversity of Shane MacGowan's personal challenges were remarkable. MacGowan, an Irish immigrant living in England when he was born on Christmas Day in 1957, had to navigate the challenges of identity. His early years of cultural exile and social difficulties laid the groundwork for a turbulent life filled with highs and lows.

His experience with substance abuse, especially alcohol, started at a young age. It turned into a guide through the rough seas of his developing music career and personal life. The difficulties

MacGowan encountered—such as cultural isolation and the demands of celebrity—created a perfect storm that fueled the turbulent periods in his life.

THE DARK MUSE: ABUSE OF SUBSTANCES AS A CREATIVE CATARACT

Substance misuse turned into more than just a battle for MacGowan; it became a sinister inspiration that spurred his artistic spark. He saw the world through the highs and lows of addiction, which helped him to distil his experiences into moving lyrics that spoke to listeners with an unvarnished realism.

MacGowan's music has a cathartic quality since it can transcend the present difficulties and serve as a medium for expression. His lyrics' unadulterated emotion frequently reflected the severity of his own struggles, forging an emotional bond between the performer and his listeners. MacGowan discovered a source of inspiration in the shadowy reaches of addiction, turning suffering into art.

AVAILABILITY SHOWED: THE ACTUALITY OF MACGOWAN'S LYRICS

Shane MacGowan's Melody: A Journey Through the Punk-Folk Symphony

MacGowan's lyrics reveal a vulnerability that is at the core of his catharsis. His poems on love, grief, and social issues were more than just lyrical observations; they were mirror images of his real-life experiences. His battles with drugs and alcohol turned into a recurring theme, casting a shadow over his poetic landscape paintings.

In tunes such as "Rainy Night in Soho," MacGowan's moving lyrics encapsulate the essence of individual grief and healing. His lyrics' vulnerability draws listeners into the private passages of his soul, going beyond simple confession. By sharing his personal scars, MacGowan established a cathartic environment where others could relate to his suffering and find comfort in the common challenges he skillfully incorporated into his stories.

SELF-REFLECTION VIA MUSIC: TRAVERSING THE ADDICTION'S LABYRINTH

MacGowan used music as a mirror for introspection and as a way to make sense of the maze that is addiction and how it affected his life. Songs such as "The Sick Bed of Cuchulainn" convey a sense of reckoning, an acceptance of mortality and the fallout from a turbulent way of life.

In certain moments, the catharsis becomes a kind of self-interrogation rather than just an outlet for emotion. MacGowan uses song lyrics as a tool for introspection while he battles his own personal issues. The stage, where the most raw vulnerability is displayed, becomes a confessional booth where people can share and personally go through a cathartic process.

IMPACT ON ARTISTIC VISION AND PERFORMANCE: THE COST OF CATHARSIS

The cost of catharsis is starkly illustrated by the toll that substance misuse has taken on MacGowan's physical well-being and live performances. His off-stage troubles were evident in his mobility issues and fractured relationships within the band.

However, performing continued to be a therapeutic experience. Despite its difficulties, the stage turned into a haven where MacGowan could momentarily escape the constraints placed on him by personal hardships. The line between performer and audience grew hazy during intense live performances, and the cathartic emotional interchange proved to be evidence of the music's transformational potential.

LEGACY AMID TURMOIL: MACGOWAN'S ARTISTRY'S LASTING IMPACT

Punk-folk culture has been profoundly impacted by Shane MacGowan's complicated relationship with personal issues, substance misuse, and the therapeutic quality of his work. His influence reaches listeners' hearts who find solace in the genuineness of his work, transcending the turbulent periods of his life.

The capacity of MacGowan's talent to transform suffering into beauty is what gives it its lasting influence. His compositions are timeless narratives that encapsulate the universal problems of the human condition, in addition to being reflections of personal suffering. By embracing the healing potential of music, MacGowan left behind a legacy that reaches beyond the turmoil of his personal experience and provides comfort and empathy to anyone navigating their own maze of hardships.

The intricate connection between Shane MacGowan's drug misuse, personal hardships, and the cathartic quality of his music

Shane MacGowan's Melody: A Journey Through the Punk-Folk Symphony

creates a picture of a troubled genius whose creations evolved into a symphony of resiliency and redemption. He overcame difficult obstacles by using the transforming potential of art to help him escape the maze of addiction and tell the world about his journey. His music's therapeutic process is proof of the art form's enduring power to transform human suffering into something profoundly universal, an eternal symphony that reverberates through the annals of musical history.

Shane MacGowan's Melody: A Journey Through the Punk-Folk Symphony

CHAPTER 5:

BEYOND THE STAGE: MACGOWAN'S IMPACT ON MUSIC AND CULTURE

The cultural influence of Shane MacGowan extends beyond the music industry and into other domains such as literature, film, and social storylines. His impact has made a lasting impression on cultural landscapes, shaping views of Irish identity, punk subculture, and the meeting point of tradition and rebellion. It was formed by the merger of punk ethos, folk traditions, and unadulterated storytelling.

1. Redefining Irish Identity: The lyrics by MacGowan serve as a type of modern Irish literature. His songs' integration of Irish history, folklore, and urban realities creates a distinctive narrative thread that adds to the changing fabric of Irish identity in the contemporary era.

MacGowan's music subverted preconceived ideas about Irish cultural expression by fusing punk with folk. It redefined how the world views and interacts with Irish identity by offering a colourful, rebellious alternative to traditional Irish music.

2. Punk Ethos and Subversion: MacGowan's anti-establishment attitude is embodied in his lyrics and way of life, which are strongly rooted in the punk ethos. His defiant style challenges conventional wisdom and conventions, adding to the punk subculture's revolutionary story.

MacGowan introduced a dash of defiance into popular culture with The Pogues' music. The group broke down barriers and impacted a new generation of musicians with their unreserved blending of genres and investigation of forbidden subjects.

3. Cinematic Impact: A cinematic examination of Shane MacGowan's life is presented in the 2020 documentary "Crock of Gold: A Few Rounds with Shane MacGowan". The movie explores the artist's cultural significance beyond just his music, providing a complex portrait of the musician as a cultural icon. The life story of MacGowan, as told in documentaries and possibly as a source of inspiration for upcoming motion picture projects, becomes a cultural saga that goes beyond music. Through its exploration of issues like creativity, resilience, and the meeting point of individual problems with larger societal dynamics, it represents the complexity of the human experience.

4. Social Commentary and Storytelling: MacGowan frequently captures the grim realities of city life in his lyrics, using urban realism as a technique. This narrative technique offers social criticism by providing a glimpse into the challenges faced by common people and the effects of societal shifts on personal life.

His skill in combining aspects of grim urban life, Irish folklore, and introspective thoughts results in a narrative tapestry that speaks to a wide range of listeners. This narrative goes beyond music and adds to a larger conversation about culture.

5. Influence on Contemporary musicians: MacGowan's inventive combination of punk and folk continues to inspire modern musicians nowadays. The ever-changing panorama of alternative and folk-influenced genres is shaped by this musical history.

MacGowan's inventive storytelling transcends musical genres and inspires musicians who aim to incorporate unconventional storytelling into their work. His influence on storytelling skills and lyricism can be seen in artists who work at the nexus between modernity and tradition.

6. Legacy as a Cultural Icon: MacGowan has become a symbol of authenticity thanks to his life narrative and artistic development. His reluctance to live up to expectations is a potent emblem of uniqueness and self-expression, both in his musical career and personal life.

MacGowan becomes an archetype in the larger cultural context, a person whose life and contributions capture the hardships and victories of a particular time period. The cultural narratives surrounding creativity, authenticity, and identity are shaped in part by his legacy.

The influence of Shane MacGowan on culture is not limited to the music business. As a cultural trailblazer, he has reinterpreted Irish identity, questioned accepted wisdom, and evolved into a representation of sincerity and fortitude. MacGowan's impact spans a wide range of cultural contributions that continue to influence how we view and interact with the intersections of music, identity, and storytelling, from the punk-folk uprising to his influence on cinematic tales.

Shane MacGowan's unabashed genuineness and renegade persona had an impact on fashion, lifestyle, and social conventions in addition to the music industry. His unique look, which combined folk influence with punk irreverence, came to represent nonconformity, subverting social mores and influencing attitudes in the community:

Shane MacGowan's Melody: A Journey Through the Punk-Folk Symphony

1. Iconoclastic Fashion: MacGowan's ensembles of ragged garments, unique pieces, and disdain for traditional fashions embodied the punk spirit. His punk-folk fusion gave his appearance a unique visual identity, reflecting the wide range of styles in his music.

MacGowan's clothing reflected the do-it-yourself (DIY) ethos of punk culture, which was anti-establishment. His clothing evolved into a vehicle for his personal style, prioritising uniqueness over prevailing fashions.

2. Cultural Nonconformity: MacGowan's persona disregarded clichéd depictions of Irish nationality. The combination of traditional Irish characteristics and punk rebellion subverted expectations and aided in the general cultural transition away from inflexible stereotypes.

His unreserved honesty embraced individualism and exhorted others to value their own identities. The celebration of nonconformity and variety has a knock-on effect on social standards, promoting tolerance and inclusivity.

3. Lifestyle as a Statement: MacGowan personified the anti-hero image with his anti-conventional norms-disregarding lifestyle. His open battles with drug misuse and disobedience to social norms evolved into a defiant manifesto against conformist ideology.

MacGowan's way of life had a countercultural influence that went beyond the music industry. It added to a larger societal dialogue of what constitutes success, the cost of notoriety, and the acceptability of nontraditional lives.

MacGowan's impact was felt by subcultures that embraced the combination of punk and folk aesthetics. This merging not only affected musical genres but also permeated subcultures that emphasised nonconformity's visual character.

Subcultures where people attempted to craft their own stories were impacted by the do-it-yourself mentality that MacGowan personified. This method was also used in fashion, promoting the rejection of mass-produced looks in favour of unique, handmade creations.

4. Redefining Beauty Standards: MacGowan defied conventional notions of beauty with her unusual features. His genuineness and reluctance to adhere to traditional beauty standards helped to redefine beauty in the context of culture. The obvious effects of MacGowan's lifestyle decisions on his looks sparked a movement in society to accept flaws as a sign of beauty. Those who were looking for more authentic portrayals in media and fashion found resonance in this break from airbrushed perfection.

5. Cultural icon of Rebellion: MacGowan became a cultural icon of rebellion due to his unabashed sincerity and rebellious persona. His defiance of social conventions came to represent people who are opposing the existing quo in a variety of spheres of life.

His influence on teenage culture is demonstrated by the enduring infatuation with punk aesthetics and disregard of conventional norms. MacGowan continues to be a source of inspiration for people looking for different ways to represent who they are.

Beyond the music industry, Shane MacGowan's unreserved authenticity and renegade persona have left a lasting legacy. His impact on society conventions, dress, and lifestyle is proof of the ability of nonconformity to affect attitudes in a community. MacGowan's influence endures because of his rejection of stereotypes, celebration of individualism, and anti-establishment demeanour. These qualities encourage others to embrace authenticity and chart their own routes outside of social norms.

The lasting legacy that MacGowan cultivated both inside and outside of the Pogues, as well as his impact on succeeding generations of musicians.

Shane MacGowan's reputation as a musician goes far beyond his time as The Pogues leader, and he has had a significant impact on several generations of musicians. His influence on the music industry is marked by an uncompromising genuineness, a raw narrative style that blends punk and folk, and a unique synthesis that has impacted the trajectory of several genres and inspired a new wave of artists worldwide:

1. Pioneering Punk-Folk Fusion: MacGowan created a style that defied genres with his groundbreaking work with The Pogues, fusing punk intensity with traditional folk tunes. Not only did this combination bring folk music back to life, but it also created opportunities for experimentation in other musical genres.

The rise of bands and musicians that take inspiration from MacGowan's ability to unite seemingly incongruous genres to create a musical tapestry that resonates across cultural boundaries is evidence of the global effect of The Pogues' punk-folk fusion.

Shane MacGowan's Melody: A Journey Through the Punk-Folk Symphony

2. Storytelling Excellence: MacGowan's skill as a lyricist elevated songwriting to a craft, distinguished by vivid storytelling and raw emotion. His skill at crafting complex stories within the parameters of a song has established a benchmark for musicians who want to use their music to convey powerful tales to future generations.

MacGowan's effect on the folk revival movement is evident. His storytelling methods, which frequently draw from urban realism and Irish folklore, have inspired modern folk artists who want to add narrative depth to their pieces.

3. Cultural Relevance and Authenticity: MacGowan defied convention by representing his Irish identity authentically and by refusing to fit in with conventional wisdom. Genuine expression is valued in a cultural movement that is fueled by artists that aspire to defy industry norms and find resonance in this honesty. Beyond The Pogues, MacGowan's reputation of honesty has influenced musicians that value authenticity above all else in their musical pursuits. His influence is seen in the growth of artists who put authentic storytelling ahead of business concerns.

4. Diverse Genre Influence: Mackowian's impact transcends genre boundaries. It resonates with musicians in a variety of genres, including punk, folk, rock, and alternative. His method of pushing boundaries inspires musicians to venture into uncharted sound realms.

MacGowan's embodiment of the punk ethos has transcended its original environment, inspiring artists to rethink and interpret punk values in modern contexts. With every generation of musicians, punk-folk's lasting impact keeps changing.

5. Lasting Influence on Collaborations: MacGowan's partnerships, both inside and outside of The Pogues, demonstrate his ability to mix well with musicians from many backgrounds. This spirit of cooperation has encouraged younger generations to investigate cross-cultural collaborations, resulting in a more diverse and integrated international music landscape. The long-lasting influence of MacGowan's joint endeavours has helped folk-punk fusion develop. This genre, which combines punk intensity with folk narrative, is still a thriving area where musicians are experimenting with new sound possibilities.

6. Cultural Archetype of Resilience: MacGowan's life narrative, which was characterised by hardships and victories on a personal level, has evolved into a resilient culture. This story of triumphing against adversity has struck a chord with musicians on their own journeys, inspiring tenacity and resolve.

Shane MacGowan's Melody: A Journey Through the Punk-Folk Symphony

The stories that are adopted by artists of later generations are part of MacGowan's lasting legacy. His influence is especially noticeable among artists that use music as a cathartic and self-expression medium while navigating personal problems.

Shane MacGowan left behind a timeless and complex legacy that has influenced several generations of musicians. His influence may be heard in the developing sounds of modern musicians who are influenced by his inventive musical fusion, masterful storytelling, cultural relevance, and unabashed sincerity. This influence extends beyond The Pogues. As a musical trailblazer, MacGowan has irrevocably altered the course of world music, ensuring that his legacy will always influence and motivate the artistic pursuits of those who choose to follow in his rebellious and genuine footsteps.

CONCLUSION

We find ourselves at the nexus of revelation and contemplation in the last notes of this examination of Shane MacGowan's life, songs, and legacy. Through the highs and lows, melodies and dissonances that make up the symphony of one of music's most mysterious characters, "Unveiling the Soul: A Musical Odyssey Explored" has taken readers on a voyage. Now that this journey has come to an end, it's time to combine the insights from every chapter and create a thorough picture that reveals the essence of The Pogues' frontman.

We set the scene early on in our story by providing a glance into the punk-folk scene of the late 1970s. It was a world of revolt, of clashing cultures, and of the nascent beginnings of a musical genre that would upend established conventions. After enduring this trial by fire, MacGowan became a key player in the music revolution by defying accepted wisdom and choosing a less-travelled route. His unreserved authenticity turned into a distinguishing quality, establishing the framework for a theme that developed in the following chapters.

The investigation of the soul behind The Pogues' frontman was the main theme that threaded through MacGowan's life. We

Shane MacGowan's Melody: A Journey Through the Punk-Folk Symphony

followed his early years, exploring the early encounters that moulded his creative instincts. Every chapter revealed a new aspect of MacGowan's multifaceted personality, from the sources of his rebellious spirit to the inspirations that first stoked his love of music. The origins of The Pogues and the group dynamic that characterised the band's formation demonstrated the sense of community that drove MacGowan's artistic pursuits.

We discovered the collaboration between MacGowan's brilliant lyrics and the group's musical prowess as we moved to examine his function as the captivating frontman. The Pogues' unique style was characterised by a harmonic fusion of melodies and words that danced together. The transition of this sound, from an unpolished punk-folk fusion to a polished symphony that enthralled listeners all over the world, reflected MacGowan's own artistic development.

We examined the components that made up MacGowan's poetic arsenal by dissecting the layers of his songwriting process. We looked at how his songs blended gritty urban experiences, Irish folklore, and introspective thoughts to create a narrative tapestry that spoke to a wide range of listeners. Important songs functioned as case studies, illuminating the complex network of

Shane MacGowan's Melody: A Journey Through the Punk-Folk Symphony

narratives and emotions that MacGowan incorporated into his works.

We discussed the struggles and victories that shaped MacGowan's artistic vision as we navigated through the turbulent periods of his personal life. The investigation examined the intricate connection between MacGowan's drug usage, personal hardships, and the healing power of his music. It was an incredibly resilient and vulnerable journey that demonstrated the transformational potential of creativity in overcoming the maze of personal challenges.

We learned more about the subtleties of this delicate interaction as we dug deeper into the relationship between MacGowan's personal issues, substance misuse, and the cathartic quality of his music. His life turned into a symphony of hardships, and substance misuse emerged as a creative stimulus as well as a challenge. MacGowan's music possessed a cathartic effect that extended beyond the immediate problems, serving as a genuine and real medium for expression.

By exploring resilient moments, we illuminate the unwavering spirit that propelled MacGowan's artistic endeavours. From the beginnings of The Pogues to the critical success of albums such

Shane MacGowan's Melody: A Journey Through the Punk-Folk Symphony

as "Rum, Sodomy & the Lash" and classic pieces such as "Fairytale of New York," MacGowan's capacity to transform personal anguish into innovative works of art demonstrated a fortitude that extended beyond the stage. His influence encompassed one-man projects, accolades, and a legacy documented in the film "Crock of Gold: A Few Rounds with Shane MacGowan."

Beyond the music, we investigated MacGowan's wider cultural influence. His impact helped redefine cultural norms and went beyond the confines of traditional Irish identity. MacGowan's embodiment of the punk ethos and irreverent attitude had a significant influence on tales in literature, film, and society. His life narrative became a cultural archetype, appealing to people who were looking for nonconformity and authenticity.

We discovered a cultural change by investigating the ways in which MacGowan's unabashed genuineness and rebellious image resonated through fashion, lifestyle, and social standards. His unconventional lifestyle, disdain for preconceptions, and unorthodox fashion choices subverted social standards. Subcultures were influenced by MacGowan, who also helped redefine beauty standards by accepting flaws as a kind of beauty.

Shane MacGowan's Melody: A Journey Through the Punk-Folk Symphony

As we examined MacGowan's impact on later musical generations, we saw the lasting legacy he created both inside and outside of The Pogues. His innovative punk-folk fusion, masterful storytelling, and cultural significance affected many genres and spawned a new generation of musicians around the world. The artistic collaboration, cultural influence, and thematic coherence of MacGowan's work transcended the genre and time to leave an enduring legacy.

In summary, "Unveiling the Soul: A Musical Odyssey Explored" has been an investigation of the profound rather than merely a biography. The insights from every chapter have been combined to provide a complete picture of Shane MacGowan—the man behind the song. This theme trip demonstrated the way in which MacGowan's life, songs, and legacy are interwoven in a deep investigation of identity and artistic expression. Readers come away from it with a deep admiration for Shane MacGowan's musical voyage and a deeper knowledge of the complexity that moulded this musical pioneer. His genuine narrative and rebellious spirit reverberate as we conclude this chapter, beckoning us to pay attention, consider, and enjoy the symphony that lives on in the souls of those who have embarked on this musical voyage.

Shane MacGowan's Melody: A Journey Through the Punk-Folk Symphony

Epilogue: Echoes in Time

As we draw the final curtain on "Shane MacGowan's Melody: A Journey Through the Punk-Folk Symphony," it's a moment of reflection, a pause to appreciate the harmonies and dissonances that have echoed through the pages of this biography. The symphony of Shane MacGowan's life, with its highs and lows, resonates not only in the melodies he crafted but in the indomitable spirit that defines his legacy.

Reflections on a Musical Odyssey

The narrative journey we undertook was more than a chronological retelling of events; it was an exploration of identity, resilience, and the transformative power of music. From the punk-folk landscape of the late '70s to the refined symphony that captivated global audiences, MacGowan's life became a musical odyssey, a journey marked by rebellion, collaboration, and unapologetic authenticity.

In revisiting the genesis of The Pogues and the collaborative energy that defined the band's inception, we witnessed the birth of a musical revolution. The charismatic frontman, Shane MacGowan, emerged as the voice of a generation, fusing raw lyricism with the musical prowess of the ensemble. The evolution of The Pogues' sound, from the raw punk-folk fusion to the refined symphony, mirrored MacGowan's own growth as an artist.

Peeling Back the Layers: Unmasking the Soul

Delving into the intricacies of MacGowan's songwriting process, we dissected the elements that constituted his poetic toolkit. Irish folklore, gritty urban experiences, and personal reflections converged in his lyrics, creating a tapestry of storytelling that resonated with a diverse audience. Key songs served as case studies, revealing the intricate web of emotions and narratives woven into MacGowan's compositions.

The exploration extended beyond the music to the tumultuous chapters of MacGowan's personal life. We addressed challenges and triumphs, navigating through the complex relationship between his personal struggles, substance abuse, and the cathartic nature of his music. Each revelation peeled back layers, exposing vulnerabilities and resilience that added depth to the narrative.

Shane MacGowan's Melody: A Journey Through the Punk-Folk Symphony

Cultural Impact: Beyond the Stage

Beyond the music, we explored MacGowan's broader cultural impact. His unapologetic authenticity and rebellious image reverberated through fashion, lifestyle, and societal norms. His influence challenged established ideals, contributing to a redefinition of cultural standards. The echoes of MacGowan's countercultural spirit extended beyond music, becoming a cultural archetype that resonated with those who embraced nonconformity.

Examining how MacGowan's impact transcended music, we navigated through the realms of fashion, lifestyle, and societal norms. His iconoclastic choices, rejection of stereotypes, and countercultural lifestyle became symbolic of a cultural shift. MacGowan's influence extended to subcultures and contributed to the redefinition of beauty standards, embracing imperfections as a form of beauty.

Legacy Crafted: Influence on Generations

The exploration concluded with an examination of MacGowan's influence on subsequent generations of musicians. His pioneering punk-folk fusion, storytelling excellence, and cultural

Shane MacGowan's Melody: A Journey Through the Punk-Folk Symphony

relevance left an indelible mark, transcending temporal and genre boundaries. The collaborative spirit, cultural impact, and thematic resonance of MacGowan's work became a timeless musical archetype.

In the final chapters, we explored the enduring legacy MacGowan crafted within and beyond The Pogues. His impact extended to solo endeavours, recognition in awards, and a legacy captured in the documentary "Crock of Gold: A Few Rounds with Shane MacGowan." The exploration of his influence on subsequent generations became a testament to the lasting imprint of his musical odyssey.

A Comprehensive Portrait: Synthesis of Revelations

Now, as we synthesise the revelations from each chapter, we offer a comprehensive portrait of the soul behind The Pogues' frontman. The thematic journey illustrated how MacGowan's life, lyrics, and legacy intertwined in a profound exploration of identity and art. The symphony of his existence, laid bare through the melodies, invites readers to reflect on their own journeys and appreciate the transformative power of storytelling.

Shane MacGowan's Melody: A Journey Through the Punk-Folk Symphony

Unveiling The Soul: A Musical Odyssey Explored

In conclusion, "Shane MacGowan's Melody" has been more than a biography; it has been an odyssey explored. The synthesis of revelations, the reflection on the thematic journey, and the enduring appreciation for the musical odyssey define the essence of this narrative. The epilogue is not just a closing chapter but an invitation to continue listening, to the melodies that transcend time, to the stories that resonate in the soul, and to the echoes of rebellion that reverberate through the symphony of Shane MacGowan's life.

As the author, Roland T. Owens, I extend my gratitude to every reader who embarked on this literary journey. Your curiosity, reflection, and connection with the music have breathed life into these pages. May the melodies of Shane MacGowan's life linger, and may this biography be a testament to the enduring power of storytelling.

In the spirit of exploration, reflection, and appreciation, we bid farewell to this odyssey, a journey through the punk-folk symphony that defines Shane MacGowan's legacy.

Roland T. Owens

Shane MacGowan's Melody: A Journey Through the Punk-Folk Symphony

Afterword: Resonance Beyond the Final Chord

As the echoes of Shane MacGowan's melodies linger in the air, I find myself standing at the intersection of reflection and revelation. The journey we embarked on through the pages of "Shane MacGowan's Melody: A Journey Through the Punk-Folk Symphony" has been nothing short of an odyssey, a rhythmic exploration of rebellion, passion, and the indomitable spirit that defines a musical icon.

In these concluding words, let's not just bid farewell to the biography but reflect on the resonance that extends beyond the final chord. The afterword is a celebration—a celebration of the melodies that continue to play, the stories that persist in the collective consciousness, and the enduring impact of an artist who dared to dance to his own unique tune.

The Melody Persists: A Timeless Cadence

As we close the book, the melody of Shane MacGowan's life persists. It's a timeless cadence that transcends the boundaries of genres and eras. In each note, in every lyric, there's a resonance that defies temporal constraints. The afterword becomes a moment to acknowledge that the music doesn't fade away; it evolves into a legacy—a symphony that continues to resonate in the hearts of those who have listened.

Revelling in the Stories: A Tapestry of Memories

This is a revelry, a celebration of the stories woven into the tapestry of this biography. It's a recognition that these narratives are not confined to the pages of a book. They become a part of the collective memory, a shared tapestry of experiences that bind us together. The afterword invites readers to revel in the richness of these stories, to carry them forward as threads that connect us through the love of music and the appreciation of authentic storytelling.

Beyond the Final Page: A Continuation of Discovery

The afterword extends an invitation—an invitation to go beyond the final page. The journey doesn't conclude with the last chapter; it's a continuum of discovery. The melodies of Shane MacGowan's life become a soundtrack for personal exploration. What resonates with you? What lyrics linger in your thoughts?

Shane MacGowan's Melody: A Journey Through the Punk-Folk Symphony

The afterword encourages readers to carry the spirit of exploration into their own lives, to seek resonance beyond the confines of these pages.

Dancing with Rebellion: A Call to Embrace Authenticity

In these concluding remarks, let's dance with rebellion. The afterword is a call to embrace authenticity, to step into the rhythm of your own unique melody. Shane MacGowan's life, marked by unapologetic choices and a rebellious spirit, becomes a beacon for those who dare to challenge norms. The afterword becomes a dance floor where individuality takes centre stage, and the music of authenticity plays loud and clear.

Acknowledging the Silence: Reflection on Absence

Yet, in celebrating the melodies and stories, the afterword acknowledges the silence, the spaces where notes once played but have now faded away. It's a moment to reflect on absence, to recognize that every melody has its final note. In this acknowledgment, the afterword becomes a pause—a reflective silence that pays homage to the spaces in between, where the music of Shane MacGowan's life once resided.

Shane MacGowan's Melody: A Journey Through the Punk-Folk Symphony

The Power of Connection: A Communal Applause

Finally, this is a communal applause. It's a recognition that the power of connection extends beyond the author's words to the readers who engaged with the narrative. Every turn of the page was a collective act, and every moment of reflection was a shared experience. The afterword becomes a standing ovation for the readers who brought this biography to life with their curiosity, passion, and appreciation for the artistry of storytelling.

As we step away from the closing chords of "Shane MacGowan's Melody," let the afterword linger, a catchy cadence that invites you to carry the resonance, revel in the stories, continue the discovery, dance with rebellion, acknowledge the silence, and join in the communal applause.

In the spirit of music, storytelling, and the enduring power of connection, let the afterword be a reminder that the melody doesn't truly end; it transforms into a timeless rhythm that continues to play in the hearts of those who listen.

Here's to the afterword—an encore that invites you to keep dancing to the melody of your own unique symphony.

Roland T. Owens

Shane MacGowan's Melody: A Journey Through the Punk-Folk Symphony

Printed in Great Britain
by Amazon